MW00899266

Data Analytics
What Every Business Must Know About Big Data and Data Science

James Smith

i

CONTENTS

Thank you for buying this Pinnacle Publishers Book!

Join our mailing list and get updates on new releases, deals, bonus content and other great books from Pinnacle Publishers. We also give away a new eBook every week completely free!

Scan the Above QR Code to Sign Up

Or visit us online to sign up at
www.pinnaclepublish.com/a/link/ebook-news/

Introduction

You may be the owner of a business, or someone who actively participates in the day to day operations of a business. We will go ahead and assume that your business is operating at a profit and you are happy with the direction it is going. As someone in this situation you might ask yourself, "Why do I need Data Analysis anyways?". I'll tell you why, one simple reason. You are leaving money on the table. Let's put it this way.. you are doing good, but wouldn't you rather be doing great? Wouldn't you rather have the ability to predict how the consumers in your target market are going to be behaving a year from now? Five years from now? This is where Data Analysis comes in.

Many people realize the need to pay attention to data in their business, but have no clue where to start. With the help of this book you will be better able to understand the importance of the data surrounding your business and exactly what to do with it.

Chapter 1 - The Importance of Data in Business

Today, many companies spend a lot of time and money on the collection and analysis of data, but why are they doing this and what are they benefiting from it?

Data is basically all of the information collected by a business each day. For this data to be collected, each sale must be recorded, but individual sales are not going to provide the company with much information.

However, when looked at in large groups, this data can provide companies with a ton of information. It can allow them to understand sales trends, what is making the most profit, what days of the week provide the most sales, as well as what is not selling and what days they are making the lowest profit.

Information like this can be vital when it comes to running a business. Let's say, for example, you are running a bakery and after analyzing the data, you have found that the majority of cakes are ordered on Friday, but no cakes are ordered on Monday. This will allow you to ensure you have plenty of cakes available on Friday when you know they will sell and only one or two available on Monday to reduce your losses for the day.

On top of this, by using this data, you will be able to decide if you want to run a promotion on Mondays to boost your sales on that day each week. You may also be able to cut back on the number of employees you need each Monday, because sales are so low, which will, of course, save you money in the long run.

Data has become extremely important for businesses because we live in a world that is constantly changing. This means that businesses are constantly changing as well. Because so many changes are taking place, businesses have to be able to keep up with these changes. You see, a business that is always struggling to catch up is not going to be a successful business.

You will also be able to use data to ensure that you have satisfied customers and if you find that your customers are unhappy, you will be able to make the changes necessary to keep them coming back.

In the past, most data was used by the IT team of a company, which meant that any changes that needed to take place or anything that needed to be addressed was done so behind the scenes. This often meant that a company would submit a request for a change and the IT team would handle it. Today, however, most companies want to analyze the data for themselves, and they want to have access to all of the information.

Long gone are the days when data was typed into an excel sheet and manipulated to meet the needs of the company. It was a system that really never worked because if a company is only meeting its own needs, and not the needs of the consumer, the company is not going to go very far. The types of data that businesses collect can be vast and it really depends on the type of data that is generated by the company's specific product.

Generally, most businesses will start out with numerical data. This is data that is based on numbers. For example, the number of sales per day, the number of sales per day of a specific item, the number of customers per day, money earned and spent, and the average amount of money spent per customer per visit.

This type of data is going to allow you to see where you need to improve when it comes to sales, what specific products your customers are interested in, and what products they are not interested in at all. This will also help you to ensure that you are actually earning money each day instead of losing it.

Another type of data that is collected is qualitative data. This type of data is collected directly from the customers usually via a survey. I'm sure that you have looked at a receipt at some point and noticed the little survey website listed at the bottom. Often times, this will state that there is some type of reward that can be won if the survey is filled out.

Why would companies do this? This is done so that companies can get more than just numerical data, so they can get real data from the customers who come into their business. Some companies may ask about the cleanliness of the business, if items were stocked on the shelves, if items were easy to find, and if the customer was happy with the overall experience.

Of course, not everyone is going to fill out this survey, but when a company gets 100 surveys filled out, and when analyzing the data find that 84% of the customers said that the product they were looking for was not in stock, the company now knows there is a problem with stocking or that they need to have more product on hand to satisfy their customers.

As I stated, the types of data that can be gathered is endless as is the ways that the data can be collected. This often leads companies into a trap because they feel that the more data they have, the better off the company will be.

Most data managers are spending at least two hours of their working day searching for data, however, what they are finding is that about 80% of the data they have to work with is completely useless.

This means that when data collection is taking place, companies need to be more careful about what data they are collecting. To ensure that data that is not useful is not being collected, it is important for the company to first determine what data is important to them and their company.

For example, let's say that your business is selling products on a website. Before each customer orders a product, they are asked to fill out specific questions. Although it would be great for a company selling weight loss products to know the average weight of their first time customers, it would not be important for a company selling perfume, for example.

This is where many companies become confused because after they have collected as much data as possible, they are left to sift through it and try to figure out what it means for them as a company.

To determine what information should be collected, a company should look at the top three challenges they are currently facing. The next step is to ask who should be involved in the process. Then ask if there are already any systems in place that could collect the data. Finally, you need to determine how the data will be tracked.

One of the biggest issues with data gathering is that many companies are unable to justify the cost or identify any return on their investment. If you cannot determine a return on the investment, then chances are, that bit of data does not matter.

However, if you can justify the cost by knowing that the information you are going to gather is going to help you increase sales or improve customer relations, then that is the type of data you want to gather.

To put all of this together, you want to start small. Focus on the areas of your business that you know need the most improvement. As you improve upon your data collection in those areas, you will be able to branch out into other areas, ensuring that you are collecting the right data for your business.

Study after study has found that companies are able to make huge financial gains when they use data to make small improvements in their business. By increasing the usability of the data that a business is collecting, they can increase their sales by about 15% per employee per year.

By looking at the data collected, most of the time, companies are going to find that everything is fine, but there is always going to be that one anomaly that is going to tell them there is something that can be improved upon. It is finding those anomalies that is important if a company wants the data to help them increase sales.

However, there are going to be times when a company finds that the data they are collecting is showing them that everything is, in fact, not okay and that is when the data collection is the most important because it could be what actually saves the business from going under.

By looking at the data and understanding what changes need to be made, a company can actually turn things around. However, if that company did not gather that data or never paid attention to what the data was telling them, chances are, they would not be a business much longer.

Chapter 2 - Big Data, and Its Value and Advantages

Big data is a term that is used for data that is so large that traditional applications for analyzing data are useless. However, the term big data can also be used when talking about specific advanced methods of collecting data and often does not refer to the size of the data being collected.

Big data does not take samples. In other words, big data is going to track what happens as a whole. Big data also does not focus on the 'why'. Instead, it is used to detect patterns and it is usually cost free because it is created by digital interactions that are already happening.

To put things simply, it is nothing more than huge amounts of data. This data is easy for companies to obtain, but because of the amount of data that is obtained, it is difficult for today's technology to handle it all. Often times, this data is coming in from multiple sources such as computers, satellites, and mobile devices. This can cause a problem when it comes to storing the data as well as moving it around until it can be analyzed.

There are those, however, who feel big data can cause problems, thinking that it is just another way for government and businesses to invade their privacy and gather information about them, but that is simply not what big data is used for when it comes to businesses.

When it comes to business, big data refers to information that is going to allow the company to improve their products, understand their target market, and even create new products that their consumers are looking for.

Think about Google, for example. This is a company that deals with big data on a regular basis. This data is used to ensure that you are able to find exactly what you are looking for when you use the Google search engine, but it is also used when it comes to the ads that are going to appear while you are online. By using big data, Google ensures that you are able to find the products that best match your recent searches. Even though many people find this to be an invasion of privacy, they continue to use Google and love that they can easily find what they are looking for. This is how big data works.

You see, big data is used to build a picture of you by taking small bits of information and piecing the rest together. However, it still takes people to sift through all of that information and make the appropriate decisions when it comes to that information. It is left up to time to tell if those were the right decisions.

What is the Value of Big Data?

Big data has been with us for years, even though many people think that it is a new thing, by definition, we know that it has been around as long as computers have. You see, since man made the first computer, data collection has pushed the limits of those computers. This has led to more advanced technology or computers that are able to process more data in a shorter amount of time.

Chances are, data collection is always going to push the limits when it comes to technology, but that is simply how big data works.

Studies have shown that those companies that have been able to collect big data and use it efficiently are reaping the benefits. In other words, it is big data that is allowing many companies to grow and become as successful as they are.

Understanding that big data is nothing new and that it has been in use for a long time allows us to understand what value it has had in the past as well as what value it currently has.

By looking at what big data's value was in the past, we are able to look at a broader set of information than if we only looked at the huge Internet companies that are leading in the field of big data today.

Discovering Patterns and Taking Action

Discovering the patterns of customers is quite interesting, but it cannot be put to use unless we are able to take some sort of action that will lead to an increase in sales or a reduction of costs.

Many people have heard the story of beer and diapers. It is a story about one large retailer that, through data mining, found that when men came into their store on Friday nights to purchase diapers, there was a high percentage of them purchasing beer as well.

This allowed the company to change the layout of the store, so that they could place the beer next to the diapers. When the company did this, they found that the amount of beer they sold increased dramatically.

Once said to be a true story, it is believed to be an urban legend, but it can still help us today to understand how important data mining really is. You see, although this little nugget of information could have easily been overlooked, a pattern was discovered through big data, an action was taken, and profits increased.

In the example above, the information that was obtained was used to identify a previously unknown group of customers, men who purchase diapers on Friday night, then use the information gathered about this specific group and increase sales.

Today, the same type of information is being gathered and used. However, with the data that is available today, companies are able to focus on very narrow groups of people to ensure their profits are boosted.

Inventing Processes

Another way that big data adds value to companies is it allows them to invent processes or improve upon existing processes to improve their business. One example of this is when businesses used to have to track all of the product by hand and after all of this tracking, they would have to place orders for more product.

Then came the time that data was used to place the order. It became apparent to companies that it was easy for them to track what was being purchased and in what quantities through what was scanned on the register. Of course, because the item was sold, it was taking away from what they had in stock, therefore, they were able to use the numbers they obtained from registers to place their orders.

Today, many companies do not even have to do this, they simply decide how much of which product they need to keep in stock and when it comes time to order, their computer spits out a paper telling them exactly what to order and in what quantity. Other companies never have to worry about ordering anymore because it is all automated and they receive the amount of product they need based off of their previous sales.

All of this took place because of the data that was able to be collected, a process was improved upon, and now we have much simpler processes than we once did, at least in terms of retail business.

Advantages of Using Big Data

You may be sold on the idea of big data helping you to understand your customers, but any data can do that. This may leave you asking what the advantages of big data are.

1. Allows a dialogue with consumers.

Today's consumers are tough. They do a lot of research before they make a purchase, they ask their friends about their purchases, they want to be treated a certain way, and they want companies to truly be thankful that they chose to purchase from them.

Big data allows businesses to have an almost one-on-one conversation with their customers. Of course, this does not mean that businesses are going around having a one-on-one conversation with every single customer they have but take, for example, Company A. This company has a member's reward card that members scan before making their purchases.

This allows the workers to immediately know what the customers purchase on a regular basis and it helps the business know what types of up-sales can be made to any specific customer.

This can also allow companies to know that they may be able to sell a specific product to their customer based on what they have been searching for online as well as what they have been posting on social media. For example, if one customer posts that they want a phone with great signal, but that they are not willing to pay the high prices that comes with a contract phone, this information might allow a company to offer this specific customer a prepaid cell phone the next time they come into the store.

2. Redevelopment of your products.

By using big data, you are going to be able to understand what aspects of your product people like and what aspects people think need improved upon. You can also find out how different groups of your consumers feel about your products. For example, a stay at home mom may not feel that your product is meeting her needs while the mom who works outside of the home feels that your product makes her life much easier.

3. Perform a Risk Analysis.

By using big data, you will be able to understand what your risks will be if you, for example, change a product.

4. Big data also allows you to look at the data in real time. This means you do not have to rely on information that could be days or weeks old, but instead, you can keep up with the trends as they are happening.

5. Allows you to have the ability to identify important information that is going to help improve the quality of the decisions being made.

Although it can seem complex and hard to understand, big data can provide many benefits for many benefits. The benefits mentioned above prove that big data delivers the value companies are looking for. However, there are still a few issues, like when it comes to how big data is going to evolve, but that does not mean that this is the time to question the value of big data. In fact, that time has come and gone.

Many companies have proven that big data is able to successfully help to reduce costs, improve decision making, and even help companies improve upon already existing products while helping them to create new products.

It is clear that this era of big data is going to provide huge business opportunities, and it is important that businesses do not wait too long before taking advantage of big data.

Chapter 3 - How to Handle and Manage Big Data

Because most errors when it comes to data are human errors and not errors in the data, it would seem that the easiest way for you to handle big data is to do so by using technology instead of relying on humans to avoid having incorrect data and possibly experiencing losses.

However, this is much easier said than done but that does not mean that it is impossible. The sheer volume and variety of big data often poses problems for companies because they are unsure of how to put the data to work for them. You see, most businesses understand that there is a large amount of data and they understand that it can create a lot of value, but they are not sure where they are supposed to start.

In this chapter, I want to discuss how manage this large amount of data, which is provided to you from several sources, often times including social media as well as other online communities.

1. Think about the goals of the business before you begin collecting and analyzing data. The data that is going to be collected, especially if it is data that is unstructured, which is the type that you will collect from social media, can be extremely overwhelming and provide very little value to you if you are unsure how you are supposed to use it. Even though most companies that have a data management problem know it, they still have no clear defined plan to allow them to solve the problem. If you take the time to think about your goals in your business before you begin collecting data, you will be able to use the data to improve your business. Your goals should tell you what you want to do with the data, how you want it to be analyzed, and what problems you want the data to solve. Having a plan is going to ensure that you get the most out of big data.

2. Do not try to move the data. Many companies try to move the data around, but you have to remember that this data is current data, and there is a lot of it. When you move the data, it is going to make it unavailable to those who need it most. By the time the data is available, it is irrelevant and you will have an entirely new set of data to examine.

3. Businesses also need to make sure that they are not duplicating data. Many companies make copies of data, but the problem is that this data is not updated on a regular basis. This means that when the data is looked at later, it is out of date. Instead of making duplicates of the data, simply ensure that the data you are looking for is located in a place where you can readily find it.

4. If a company finds that the data they are gathering is simply too much and is overwhelming, it can become very easy to give up and stop using big data but if this happens, the company is actually losing out. Instead of giving up, data sampling can be used. Of course, this raises the question as to whether or not data sampling is going to decrease the chances of improving the business and the answer simply is that even though sampling is not going to include all of the data available, it is still going to use a large part of it. Using some of the data is always better than not using any of it at all.

5. Companies also have to know how to index the data they gather. If employees are looking for specific data and are unable to find it, the data collection is doing no good. If an employee cannot find the data, chances are, they are going to stop looking for the data and this means that the data is doing no good for the company. However, if proper indexing is used, the data will be accessible, ensuring that the company will benefit from it.

6. Each business has to know how to interpret the data that has been collected. Think about the company in the beer and diapers story. If the company had not known how to interpret the data they had collected properly, they might not have understood that it was men who were purchasing diapers on Friday night who were also increasing their beer sales on that night. Therefore, they could have missed out on making a ton of money.

Understanding how to manage big data is the most important thing you need to know when it comes to using big data to improve your business. Managing big data is ensuring that it is organized in a way that will ensure it is usable, ensuring that large amounts of both structured and unstructured data is accessible for business intelligence and ensuring that businesses are able to locate the valuable information that is needed.

It must be understood that most big data involves many terabytes of information and that it is saved in many different forms. This information is so vast, it cannot simply be kept on a regular 64 gigabit computer.

Chapter 4 - The Process of Data Analysis

What is Data Analysis?

Data analysis is a term used to describe the process used to evaluate data that has been collected to obtain information, form conclusions, and help to support decision making in business. This is an extremely important process if a business wants to continuously improve and make well informed decisions concerning what will happen in the future of the business.

When data is analyzed, each component is examined, then used to form some type of conclusion and most businesses understand that handling the data analysis properly will allow them to get the most out of the data, ensuring they are making the right decisions.

The Process of Data Analysis

Data analysis is the breakdown of a huge amount of data into smaller compounds that can then be examined. When data analysis takes place, it begins with obtaining the data, and then it is examined and converted into information that can be used for decision making.

This data is collected with a specific purpose in mind, either to prove a hypothesis and test theories or to answer questions.

The first step in data analysis is understanding the requirements for the data. Before data is ever collected, a business must decide what data they need to collect. The company will need to decide what questions they are trying to answer with the data that will be collected.

The second step in data analysis is the collection of the data. It is important for the data to be collected from several different sources and it needs to be specific data that will focus on the questions that need answered as determined in the first step.

Once the data is collected, it is time to process it. Data processing is what takes place when the raw data collected is converted into information that is meaningful to the company. Often times, data will be manipulated to produce results that are supposed to lead to an improvement in the business or resolution of the specific problem that initiated the data collection in the first place.

This often means that the data is placed in rows and columns, often in statistical software. After this, information is fed into the software to produce the information companies are looking for.

Once the data has been processed, it is then cleaned, which is done simply to prevent as well as correct any errors. This is done because after the data has been processed, it may be filled with gaps, can be found as incomplete, or it can be found to contain errors. Data cleaning is often done by record matching and ensuring that there is no duplicate information. Because there is such a large amount of data being processed, it is vital for the data to be cleaned. The first technique that can be used for data cleaning is called data profiling. This is done by looking at the data, and understanding the minimum and maximum values as well as the types of data in each field. By understanding these values, it becomes easier to identify data that contains quality issues as well as those that have been misunderstood.

The second technique that can be used for data cleaning is to manipulate the data by making small changes; for example, changing all of the letter O's to the number 0, or even just removing spaces within the information.

The next technique is simply ensuring that the data has been entered into the proper field. For example, it is not unheard of for a zip code to be entered into the wrong field when the data is sorted by a computer. It is also important to look at small details such ensuring that specific names such as Sam are identified as a nickname for a male named Samuel. Checking for small mistakes made by the software is very important when it comes to cleaning up the data.

Another mistake in data that needs to be looked at when cleaning data is taking place is spelling. For example, wherever and where ever to a human look to mean the same thing, but to a computer, these are completely different words and this can change the way the data is interpreted.

The next step is exploratory data analysis, which is simply looking at the data sets and determining the main characteristics. The main function of exploratory data analysis is to help businesses understand what can be learned from the data beyond any hypothesis or theory used to first initiate the data collection.

After the exploratory data analysis, models will be created to determine if by taking a specific action, a specific outcome would result. For example, in the beer and diapers example, the model would have been used to determine if more beer sales would occur by moving the beer closer to the diapers.

Data product may also be used. It is simply a computer program that takes the data, and determines that if a customer buy X product, they might also be interested in Y product, based on purchased made by other customers.

This is much like the 'other customers also purchased' section on the Amazon website. Simply by looking at what customers purchase, the program is able to determine what other products they might be interested in purchasing by using a select set of data.

After the data has been analyzed, it is then reported, which can lead to feedback and further analysis. During this step, a business has to determine how they will report the results, whether it be in charts, graphs, or other forms. This depends on what the information will be used for in the future.

Chapter 5 - Predictive Analytics

The best way to determine the future is to look at the past and that is exactly what predictive analytics does. Predictive analytics works in much the same way as a car insurance company does. You see, the company will look at a set of facts, or data set, often, your age, gender, driving record, and the type of car you drive.

By looking at this data set, they can use it to predict your chances of getting into a car accident in the future. Therefore, they are able to determine if they are willing to insure you and what rate you will pay for the insurance.

Predictive analysis uses a specific data set to determine if a pattern can be found. If a pattern is found, this pattern is used to predict future trends. This is much different than other techniques used to analyze the data sets because, unlike predictive analytics, other techniques provide a business with information about what has happened in the past.

Of course, knowing what has happened in the past when it comes to understanding data is very important, but the majority of business people would agree that what is more important is understanding what is going to happen in the future.

What Types of Predictive Analytics Are There?

There are two basic types of predictive analytics. The first is the type that is based off of variables, for example, sales on any given day, the satisfaction of customers, and losses and gains. The second type of predictive analytics is based on binary outcomes, for example, we are about to lose this customer, why a purchase was or was not made, and whether or not a transaction was fraudulent.

In companies that use predictive analytics, it has been found that they are using this process mostly for marketing and increasing sales, however, predictive analytics can be used in any of the major processes of business.

1. Smooth Forecast Model.

In this model, a business will use the variables collected, whether it be a large or small number of variables, believed to impact the specific event that is being looked at. For example, if your specific event is the increase in beer sales, you would look at the variables you believe are impacting these sales. Of course, you can use this to predict much more complex scenarios such as how well a product will sell based on the sales of similar products, if sales will increase or decrease over time, and even customer satisfaction. This is the simple way to use predictive analytics; it is easy to understand and the data can easily be manipulated.

2. Scoring Forecast Model.

This model for predictive analytics is a bit more complex than the smooth forecast model. This is a model in which data is collected and is translated into a 1 or a 0, which is why this is often referred to as a binary model.

Let's say, for example, you are trying to determine the likelihood of a specific set of customers switching to your product instead of the product they currently use.

You will first gather the information that you have about these customers, like age, where they are from, how many people live in the household, and so forth. By using the scoring forecast model, you will be able to determine the likelihood of future customers switching to your product by examining the customers who have already switched. After this is done, you will be able to give them a score, say from 1 to 10, determining the likelihood of them switching to your product from a competitor's product.

Predictive analytics does not have to be complicated and it can be one of the most important benefits of data collection. There are also two other systems for predictive analytics, the SQL and the RDBMS systems.

These are newer systems and although they are good programs, they are not perfect, only providing companies with about 80% accuracy. Of course, this is better than just guessing but there are better ways of using predictive analytics right now. However, when it comes to dealing with big data, these may have their advantages.

3. Natural Language Processing.

The process of NLP, also known as Sentiment Analysis, is used to pull data from unstructured data such as social media. This application is used to help understand how customers feel about specific products or services based on the words and phrases pulled from social media comments, for example.

Comments such as "Not worth the price", "Great service", "Waste of money", or "It broke right after we got it" are all the types of comments that will allow a company to understand how their customers feel about their products. It will also help them to understand what they need to do to ensure their customers' happiness, and based off of these comments, it can be predicted as to how well a product will do.

This type of processing can also be used for customer service calls, even as they are happening, based on the key words the company is looking for.

Of course, natural language processing is not going to give you the same accuracy as other models because you will be looking for specific key words, which could make it seem as if there are many more unsatisfied customers than there are satisfied customers, but it is going to allow you to have some insight concerning the direction you want to take your company. It can also allow you to find ways to up-sell other products. For example, if you were to look for the term, "I wish it came with", you will begin to understand what your customers are looking for and be able to offer it to them.

Each of these techniques, if used properly, can improve the finances of any company, and help them understand not only what the future may hold based on the past but also what their customers are really looking for. At this point, if a company has not gotten involved in predictive analytics, they are really missing out on important information that they really need.

Chapter 6 - Predictive Analytics Techniques (I.e., Regression Techniques and Machine Learning Techniques)

Predictive analytics is currently being used by many different companies all over the world to turn collected data into valuable information. Because the predictive analytic techniques are able to learn from the past to predict the future, more and more companies are finding them useful when it comes to their business.

There are countless predictive analytics techniques that are used every day by different businesses, many of them created specifically to support one particular business, however, there are several techniques that are generic and can be used by almost all companies.

1. Linear Regression - To understand linear regression, we must first start with linear models. Let's first begin with a mathematical model, which is simply a mathematical expression used to describe the relationship between measurements. For example, if the price of your product is $10, and you wanted to find out the price for several of your products, you would write a mathematical model like this: y=10*x with X being the number of products.

    A linear model is simply a mathematical model that contains an independent variable and a dependent variable such as our model of y=10*x. This means that no matter what x equals, y is going to be the total price for the product sold.

    What if you have to deal with shipping and handling? Let's say, for example, that your pricing is to include a shipping and handling fee of $20. You would now create a pricing model of y= 20+(10*x)

    Linear models are simply a mathematical model that is going to make linear regression easy to interpret. Linear regression is used when you do not know the parameters or your linear model. This linear model is determined through analysis and the linear regression is used to complete this.

Linear regression is used to scan the data that you do have and use that information to compute the parameters that fits best within that data. Let's say, for example, you want to predict the amount of cattle that will be born on small dairy farms. Each farm uses the same basic practices, is located in the same general area, and the only difference is the size of the farm. This leads you to believe that the size of the dairy farm is the most important piece of data when it comes to predicting the number of calves that will be born. The linear model you will create using the size of the farms is going to give you what is known as the linear regression line.

This will show you the number of calves you can expect to be born just by using the information you entered. Of course, this is not taking other information into account, such as the total number of cows on each farm, and other data that could be collected.

This is a very basic way of using predictive analytics and it is usually the first technique that is used when it comes to predictive analytics. However, because not all of the data that is available is being used, this often leads to incorrect assumptions.

2. Decision trees - This technique is a very popular data mining technique, and is liked by analysts because of the user friendly results it produces. Let's look at an example of a credit card company. Credit card companies have 2 types of customers, those who are profitable and those who are not profitable.

Customers who always pay their bills on time and in full, or do not use their credit card are not profitable customers. However, customers who have a balance on their cards or do not pay the balance in full each month are the customers who are profitable for the credit card company. Customers who do not pay their payments on time are also profitable for the company.

For this example, we will assume that this credit card company has a total of 10 customers, 5 who are profitable and 5 who are not profitable. This is what is described as the company's customer base. However, outside of this customer base is a huge number of potential customers.

The credit card company does not know if these potential customers will be profitable customers, but because there is a limited marketing budget, meaning that the company can only market to a limited number of these potential customers, the company wants to make sure that the budget is used in a manner that will ensure the company is able to attract the maximum amount of profitable customers possible.

In other words, the company wants to ensure that they are only marketing to those customers who are likely to be profitable if they become the credit card company's customers. This leads to the problem of the company being able to predict if a person is going to be profitable or not. This is where analytics come in.

The credit card company is going to have information available to them about their potential customers, such as age, gender, the number of credit cards they already own, and their marital status. The credit card company needs to find out if any of this data can help them predict if a potential customer is going to be profitable or not.

Because the same information is available to the credit card company about their existing customers. At the top of the decision tree, the company is going to find that 50% of their customers are profitable and 50% are not. This will branch off into two segments, for example, we will go with the age variable for this example, those who are 35 and older will go in one segment and those who are 34 and under in the second segment. The company will then examine the profitability rate of the two segments.

Now let's say that out of the customers who are over 35, six of them are profitable and 2 are unprofitable, giving us a profitability rate of 66%.

Once this information is compared with the overall profitability rate of 50%, the company can determine that people who are 35 and older tend to be more profitable for them than the younger group.

This allows the company to understand that if they are marketing their credit card only to people who are 35 and older, they will end up with a more profitable group of customers.

This segment will then be segmented into smaller groups, which will show an even higher profitability using the information provided such as marital status and sex.

Following this technique will allow the company to determine exactly what group of people they need to market to in order to increase the profitability of their customer base.

Machine Learning - This process is very similar to data mining, in that, like data mining, it searches through data looking for patterns. However, instead of searching for data that is going to help a person or a company understand trends, machine learning searches for data that will help to improve the program itself.

Think about Facebook's Newsfeed. This program looks for patterns, such as one person interacts often with another, likes their posts, or writes on the other person's wall. Using machine learning, Facebook assumes that the two people are close and more of that friend's posts will appear on the person's news feed.

In other words, machine learning is used in predictive analytics just as any other techniques are used, by extracting large amounts of data, assessing risk, and predicting a customer's behavior by looking at how they have behaved in the past.

There are, of course, many other techniques that can be used when it comes to predictive analytics, each advantages and disadvantages. It may take a few attempts for a company to find the technique that works best for them, but the payoff is definitely worth the work.

Chapter 7 - Why Use Predictive Analytics?

It is important to understand that predictive analytics are not going to tell you what is going to happen, but it is going to help you understand what is likely to happen. There is absolutely no way to know for sure what is going to happen in any business, or any area of life for that matter, but by using predictive analytics, we can determine what is most likely to happen if the patterns continue on into the future as they have in the past.

Reasons to Use Predictive Analysis:

1 Predictive analysis is going to allow you to compete better. Studies have shown that companies that use predictive analysis are better able to compete with other companies because they are able to use the data they already have to find out why their customers are choosing them. This allows them to correct mistakes of the past, focus on their strengths, and predict what the outcomes will be with some certainty.

2 Predictive analysis allows companies to better understand how to meet the demand of their customers. It allows companies to understand what the demand for their products are, including specific items and specific times. Companies are able to determine when they will see a large amount of sales versus a small amount of sales, which allows deliveries and staffing to be adjusting appropriately.

3 Predictive analytics allows companies to exceed the expectations of their customers. Even though it is important for companies to be able to predict customer demand, what is even more important is ensuring that you are able to keep the customers returning and this is only possible when you exceed

their expectations. One of the ways this can be done is by offering your products and services to your customers at the right time. When you are able to understand the customers' buying habits, you will be able to offer them the products they need even before they know they are going to need them. In other words, it allows you to focus not only on what the customer is looking to purchase at the moment, but also what they are going to need in the future.

4   Predictive analytics can help companies increase their efficiency. By analyzing that existing data, companies can predict if they will have any issues when it comes to supply, and even where and when production problems may occur as it pertains to the launching of a new product. Knowing ahead of time allows companies to take the steps needed to avoid these problems, therefore, increasing efficiency.

5   Predictive analytics can also help companies become better at reaching new clients. By understanding when and how customers are first contacting your company, this can be used to determine the most likely time that customers will be on, for example, social media or even when they will be willing to read emails you send to them.

Benefits of Using Predictive Analytics:

The amount of data available to businesses every day is exploding and that makes it very important for businesses to be able to turn that data into usable information. Of course, this means that if a company uses the correct processes such as predictive analytics, they will benefit in many ways. In this section, we are going to go over a few of the benefits of using predictive analytics.

1   Predictive search can be used to determine what a customer is looking for or is interested in based on what they have clicked on previously and what they have searched for in the past. This will help to increase sales by ensuring that the potential customers are able to find exactly what they are looking for or exactly what they need.

2   Of course, this will lead to recommendations and promotion of products to customers who are likely to be interested in the specific product. By using predictive analytics and machine learning, this once very complicated task becomes much easier. The customer's behavior, such as previous purchases and product searches are taken into consideration as well as the actions of other customers who searched for similar products. This allows the program to recommend products to customers based on the likelihood of them purchasing them.

3   By using predictive analytics, a company can ensure that they are offering the best price for their products and services. Data is collected from many different sources, as it pertains to a specific product, price points, and the amount of that product being sold at a specific price point. Amazon uses this technology on all of their products, and because of this, they are able to understand that although they may be able to sell a black shirt for $19, they are able to sell the same shirt in grey for $24, which, of course, by doing this, boosts their profits.

4   When you use predictive analytics, you are going to be able to better manage your supply and demand. We talked about this early on in the book when we talked about the bakery. By understanding that your demand for cakes is higher on Friday nights, you are able to ensure that you have enough supply to meet the demand. However, by knowing that the demand is low on Monday for cakes, you are able to reduce your supply, ensuring you are also reducing waste.

Even though predictive analytics can be extremely beneficial to companies, it is important for the data to have been tested, retested, and tested again before any actions are taken. It needs to be looked at in real world scenarios and even though some of the results may not seem to be correct, it is worth testing them. Who would suspect that men purchasing diapers would also purchase large amounts of beer at the same time?

Predictive analytics is just one way for us to use big data to benefit our companies but it is a very important technique that everyone should be using.

Chapter 8 - What is Data Science and a Data Scientist?

Data science is a term used to describe the process in which data is studied so that a conclusion can be made, based on the data studied. Data science is a broad term used to describe different techniques and processes that look for patterns and trends in data, which can later be used to come to some type of conclusion or hypothesis.

Data science dates back to the 1960's, when the study of data was becoming more popular. At that time, it was known as dataology, but was later deemed data science by D.J. Patil and Jeff Hammerbacher, who were chief data scientists for the U.S. government in early 2000.

Data science focuses on big data. Although it would be possible to use it to study small amounts of data, it is most generally used in large sets of data that are run through very complex processes.

Because data science is so complex, it is expensive, and because the skills that are needed are scarce in the work force, data scientists are well compensated.

Data science is used in almost every business, from nonprofit charities to the biggest insurance companies, and is not specific to one sector.

What is a Data Scientist?

A data scientist is a mathematician, a computer scientist, and a trend spotter all rolled into one. Not only that, but they are right in the middle of the business and the IT world, which means they are extremely sought after.

Just a decade ago, data scientists were not even on the radar, but because big data has become so important in recent years, they have suddenly become more popular. The huge amount of unstructured and structured data cannot be ignored, because it is a gold mine that will help to build business and increase profit as long as there is someone to do the sifting. That is where a data scientist comes in.

Where Did Data Scientists Come From?

Most data scientists started their careers as data analysts and some began as statisticians. As the use of big data began to grow, the roles of data analysts and statisticians grew as well. Gone were the days where big data was an afterthought that the IT department was in charge of handling.

It was finally understood that there was key information in the data that needed analyzed to increase profit. Soon, universities began to understand that companies wanted people who were not only team players, but who were able to analyze data, program computers, and determine trends, causing them to tweak their classes to accommodate these needs. Currently, there are more than 60 programs available in the U.S. for data scientists.

What are the Typical Job Duties for a Data Scientist?

Although there is not a conclusive job description for a data scientist, there are a few common duties that they have to complete.

1   A data scientist is in charge of collecting a large amount of information, structured and unstructured, then using techniques to analyze the data, turning it into useful information.

2   Using data to solve problems that are related to business.

3   Using programming languages such as R, SAS, and Python.

4   Having a strong understanding of statistics.

5   Ensuring that they are up-to-date when it comes to analytical techniques and that they understand how to use techniques such as machine learning.

6   Having the ability to communicate and collaborate with the IT department and management.

7   Have the ability to find patterns in data and spot trends in data that are going to benefit the business financially.

Skills You Must Have to be a Data Scientist

The term data scientist is often used as a broad term to describe several different jobs that have drastically different requirements.

There are some data scientist jobs that will require you to understand how to pull data out of a database, be an Excel master, and be able to produce charts showing the information you have found. This is a great type of job for a data scientist who is just learning the ropes, then expand their skillset.

Some jobs will consist of setting up the basic data infrastructure that the company will have to have to move forward. They will also need a person who will provide analysis for the data gathered. What you will find is that both of these jobs will be listed under Data Scientist.

A data scientist is going to find that there are, in fact, many different job descriptions for the job title but as long as they have a specific set of skills, a data scientist will not have any problem finding work.

1   A data scientist, no matter what type of job they are applying for, is going to be expected to know how to use the basic tools of the trade, for example, statistical programming language.

2   A data scientist must understand at least the basics of statistics such as maximum likelihood estimators, statistical tests, and distributions. A data scientist has to understand machine learning as well as be able to recognize when specific techniques should or should not be used.

3   Data scientists must be familiar with machine learning techniques, such as K-nearest neighbors, ensemble methods, and random forests.

4   A data scientist must be able to break down linear algebra as well as multivariable calculus equations.

5   A data scientist has to know how to handle and work with messy and incomplete data, which is, more often than not, exactly what they will be working with. This is called data munging.

6   A data scientist also has to know about data visualization and communication. This is incredibly important, because it is how others will view the data and understand it.

7   Software engineering is another skill that the data scientist must have, as well as having the ability to think like a data analysist.

Even though data science is an ill-defined field, it is one that requires much skill as well as one that many companies are in great need of right now.

Chapter 9 - How Data Science Benefits Retail

Data science benefits retailers in many ways but one of the most important ways is that it allows the retailer to put the right product in front of the right customers. Have you ever been to the same store but in different areas? Chances are, you have noticed that there are some products available in one area that are not available in other areas. Why is this?

It is because that through using data science, the businesses have been able to understand that although a specific product may be a huge seller in one area, there simply is no demand for it in another, or there is possibly a higher demand for a different type of product in the second area.

Another example is that companies are able to focus their attention on how customers come to them, online or in the physical store. This allows retailers to target specific markets when it comes to the emails they send. One example of this might be that a company will send online coupons to a specific group set of customers because they know these customers do most of their shopping online. On the other hand, they may send discounts that can be used only in the physical store to customers they know will do their shopping in the store.

Big data also allows the companies to get to know their customers' shopping habits by analyzing what they have purchased in the past. For example, if a specific group of customers is known for only purchasing a specific brand of shampoo, a retailer can send out an email to others in this same demographic, letting them know that this specific brand of shampoo is on sale, thus increasing the chances of this specific group of people becoming customers to their store.

Retailers may also find that if they place specific items near each other in the store, they are likely to sell more of both products. One example of this is the beer and diapers story. Placing women's clothing next to children's clothing is another example. You see, when a mother comes in to make a purchase for herself, and sees the children's clothing, she is more likely purchase something for her children as well.

Data science can also help retailers learn more about customer satisfaction as well as the customer's experience while in the store. This means that retailers are able to use this data to improve upon the in-store or online experience.

Data science can benefit retailers in many different ways, however, it is important for retailers to be transparent about how data is collected, what it is used for, and to address any privacy concerns.

Chapter 10 - Real World Examples of Data Science Benefitting Businesses

Wal-Mart was one of the first companies to take advantage of data science; some say that the diaper and beer story actually came from Wal-Mart. Wal-Mart used data science so that they could understand what their customers preferred in different regions. With the information they obtained, they were able to stock different locations according to what the customers wanted, which separated them from the rest of the retailers at the time.

Of course, when other companies noticed what Wal-Mart was doing as well as the success they had seen from using data science, they began using the same tactics.

At one point, the use of data science was considered a competitive edge, today, it has become more of a necessity for most businesses. It has reached the point that if a company is not using data science, they are actually at a competitive disadvantage today.

Now understanding that data science is a huge asset for businesses, many are beginning to wake up and pay attention.

Netflix is one of these companies that took notice of the importance of data science. Think about the last time you logged on to Netflix, sitting on your couch ready to enjoy your evening, you scroll through movie after move, television show after television show, once you scroll enough, you get down to the section 'Your Top Picks' and find a show that interests you. Six hours later, you can barely hold your eyes open and you wonder why you had never heard of the show before, even if it was a Netflix original. The reason... Data science.

When it comes to Netflix originals, Netflix does not have to spend tons of money to advertise, because they knew you would see the show listed in your recommendations, they also knew you would watch the show and they knew you would love it. How?

Data science allows Netflix to understand what their viewers want to watch and how they want it presented to them. Through machine learning and many other different types of data science, Netflix has become one of the most successful television streaming companies in the world today. Of course, other companies have followed Netflix but they are still leading the way.

By understanding what their viewers want to watch, Netflix is found in almost every home today, many people choosing Netflix over traditional satellite or cable television.

Netflix and other services like it use data science to understand their users' behavior. Not only are they able to track what you are interested in such as dark comedies or supernatural movies but with data science, Netflix has also been able to understand exactly what it takes for you to enjoy your shows, what the average length of credits are that you are willing to watch, and even who your favorite actors are.

One flaw that many people have noticed is that the same types of shows are recommended over and over. Let's say, for example, you watch "The Walking Dead". Everyone loves a good zombie movie or television show but with the current way data is tracked through Netflix, people who have watched "The Walking Dead" are finding nothing but zombies on their recommended list. However, Netflix seems to be quickly learning how to deal with the problem as they are diversifying the shows that are listed on the recommended lists.

Anyone who has shopped at CVS, which is a pharmacy as well as a drug store, knows that CVS uses data science to improve the shopping experience. It all starts with the customer loyalty card, which tracks every single purchase made. It supplies store coupons for the items that are purchased most often as well as coupons for items the company thinks you may be interested in.

However, what most people do not know is that CVS used data science in many other ways as well. One example of this is that they found the last mile that their drivers were driving when making deliveries to the stores was the most expensive mile of the trip. Some of their drivers were getting lost, accidents were happening, and because their drivers were getting upset, they had a high turnover rate.

After applying data science, CVS learned that 40% of the accidents that were happening with their trucks were happening at the stores. They also found that the majority of these accidents were taking place at one store in particular. CVS learned that many of their drivers were unable to figure out where they were supposed to enter the CVS store parking lots, which caused them to get lost, block traffic, and upset other drivers, and they found that it was because of this that there were so many delayed deliveries, which, of course, led to upset customers.

By gathering this data, CVS was able to improve their parking lots, where the trucks docked, focused on ensuring their drivers were happy and ensuring that the drivers knew exactly where they were going, how to enter the parking lots, and where the docks were.

By using data science, CVS was able to reduce the number of accidents their drivers were in, increase on-time deliveries, and improve their docks.

Data science is even used by your favorite fast food restaurants. For example, McDonalds. There was a time when the company only looked at the averages for each restaurant to make decisions when it came to making improvements. For example, how long it took from the time a customer ordered in the drive thru until the customer received their food and left. They also looked at what the big sellers for each store were.

With over 75 burgers being sold every second, McDonalds realized that it was important to use data science to understand what was really going on beyond just the average of each store.

By using data science, McDonalds learned not only how long it was taking customers to get through their drive thru but they learned what foods were being ordered, how large the orders were, and exactly what was holding up the line. They also began to understand what was causing customers to become upset.

One example of this was that a family would come through the drive thru, place a large order, and behind them, a single person would order a drink. The person ordering the drink would become upset because it took longer to make the family's order, thus holding them in line longer.

Therefore, by using data science, McDonalds determined when it was most likely for families to visit the drive thru, which allowed them to be prepared to fill larger orders, in a quicker period of time, ensuring that everyone was served quickly.

Grocery stores are even beginning to use data science. One particular grocery store, for instance, has found that their sales increase, not by printing a weekly flyer but by understanding exactly what their customers purchase on a regular basis.

By learning what their customers are purchasing, they are able to provide customers with coupons for items they believe the customer needs or may want. Stores implementing this new technique are reporting a much higher redemption rate than the industry average.

The data science behind this technique is quite sophisticated, and needs hundreds of data scientists pouring through several hundred terabytes of data. However, this allows these stores to know their customers better than any other stores, ensuring that they retain their customers and that they increase profits.

We have talked about Facebook, Wal-Mart, Netflix, Amazon, CVS, and grocery stores throughout this book, and how each of them have benefited from big data and data science. Hopefully, this has shown you that the benefits of data science are not restricted to just one industry but that all businesses can benefit from understanding the data.

Big data and data science are important in the real world. It is not just about gathering information and using it in pretend scenarios that may or may not happen. Instead, it is about using the data that is gathered to ultimately increase profits. This can be done by improving customer service, reducing the number of late deliveries, helping customers find exactly what they are looking for, preparing for busy periods and so much more.

Chapter 11 - Prescriptive Analytics

Business analytics is a three-part system, consisting of descriptive, predictive, and prescriptive analytics. We know that descriptive analytics focuses on what has happened in the past, predictive analytics focuses on what we believe will happen if the patterns remain the same, but prescriptive analytics focuses on determining the best solution from the available choices.

When using prescriptive analytics, a company is also able to understand how they can take advantages of future opportunities as well as understand the consequences of each possible decision.

Prescriptive analytics is also able to process new data, which allows it to increase the accuracy of the predictions that have been made, which will improve upon the quality of the decisions that are made.

Prescriptive analytics is process-intensive, which is used to analyze the possible decisions. It also focuses on what the outcomes of each decision could be and what influences each decision.

By focusing on all of this information, prescriptive analytics is able to determine what the best decision is and it is able to do this in real time. Of course, prescriptive analytics is not perfect and it is prone to the same issues as descriptive and predictive analytics such as the limitations of the data as well as external forces that are often unaccounted for when it comes to analytics.

Companies often begin by using descriptive analytics, learning how the patterns that have taken place in the past have affected the business. Once they have become well versed in descriptive analytics, they begin focusing on predictive analytics, using it to understand how they can use the patterns of the past to predict what could happen in the future of the business.

After businesses are able to use predictive analytics to understand how the past can help predict the future, they are ready to start using prescriptive analytics. This will allow them to focus on forward thinking, such as "Will this current pricing trend continue over the next three months?"

It is no wonder that the use of prescriptive analytics is on the rise, allowing many companies to gain a competitive edge over the competition. Prescriptive analytics is much more complex than predictive analytics but it can also deliver much more value to a company.

One example of this in the sales industry is that by using prescriptive analytics, a company can begin to understand their customers' preferences and use the information that is obtained to increase sales. Prescriptive analytics would allow a sales company to understand what time of day prospective customers are most likely to make a purchase when they are contacted, what type of sales or marketing strategies should be used to target the correct demographic of people, and the most appropriate product for the potential customer.

Let's look at a grocery store, for example. Of course, this is a simple example but it explains how prescriptive analytics works. For this example, we will say that Beth visits the grocery store on a regular basis and regularly purchases 2 gallons of milk each week. One week, Beth does not visit the store to purchase milk so a reminder is automatically sent to her. This process will help make Beth's life easier, and it helps the store retain a customer because she feels that they really know her as a customer and this makes her feel important.

Another example could be a dairy farm that is unable to meet the demands, and has to miss a shipment. By using predictive analytics, the farm will understand what steps need to be taken to regulate their supply, ensuring that no further shipments are missed.

Benefits of Prescriptive Analytics

When a business is able to use prescriptive analytics properly, they are able to gain insight, allowing them to increase productivity and profitability. These are just a few benefits of prescriptive analytics. Others include:

1   Allowing businesses obtain more information about their customers including what they buy and why they make those purchases.

2   Allows sales cycles to be accelerated, and companies are better able to understand cross selling.

3   Studies have shown that for every $1 spent on prescriptive analytics, the companies are able to make a profit of $10, meaning an increase in profits.

4   Prescriptive analytics helps companies to better manage their inventory, ensuring that they can reduce the amount of inventory that is stored in warehouses.

5   Automates more processes, reducing the manual processes, therefore reducing the expenses for the company.

6   Helps the company to control expenses better.

Prescriptive analytics are also able to help companies reduce their risks by allowing them to base their decisions on data, which increases the accuracy of their decisions.

Prescriptive analytics help to optimize processes, minimizing costs while ensuring that profits are maximized, thus increasing revenue for companies.

It also helps companies to identify issues within processes, faster and more precisely, as well as provides recommended actions that can be taken to improve these processes.

Most of the time, companies will focus on predictive analytics, not paying much attention to prescriptive analytics. However, these companies are missing out on some huge benefits as well as large amounts of profit.

However, companies are showing more and more interest when it comes to predictive analytics and they are beginning to understand that they are losing out by not utilizing this tool.

Even the United Postal Service have put predictive analytics to use, by focusing on cutting a few miles back on each driver's route, thus saving over 55 million dollars per year!

Prescriptive analytics is one of the ways companies can look for small changes that they can make, just as UPS did, allowing them to save millions of dollars over a short amount of time.

Utilizing prescriptive analytics should not be considered taking on a new venture or new technique when it comes to big data. Instead, it should be looked at as the final process in big data and data analytics.

You see, big data, data science, and data analytics are just like a rainbow, each of them representing a different color. You would not paint a work of art expecting to use only or two colors of the rainbow and you should not expect to be successful at using data analytics without implementing every process, such as descriptive analytics, predictive analytics, and prescriptive analytics.

Both descriptive analytics and predictive analytics are important when it comes to growing businesses today but prescriptive analytics will allow you to use the data you find by using predictive analytics to peek into the future and make the best decisions for you and your company. Passing that up is just like passing up a million dollars.

The most important part of prescriptive analytics is reducing the risks taken in any business decision and in the next chapter, we are going to focus on just that. How we can use data to reduce the risks taken when making decisions in business?

Chapter 12 - How Data Can Help Mitigate Risks in Business

Mitigating risks is an extremely important task when it comes to business and it is designed to help reduce risks or even eliminate them. This can happen by ensuring that specific events do not occur or that they are not able to impact the business.

Mitigating risk is a complex task that involves identifying the risks, assessing the risks, and prioritizing the risks, ensuring that the most threatening risks are resolved the quickest.

After a risk is identified, it is up to the risk manager to create a plan that will reduce or eliminate the risk altogether.

There are many different types of risks that have to be assessed, such as workplace accidents, loss of sales, fires, or a reduction of profits.

The point of mitigating risks is to help reduce any chances that the business might suffer a loss, protect employees, ensure customer satisfaction, and even protect the general public.

Although there are many different ways for a company to identify risks, after the risk has been identified, how big the risk is has been determine, and the expected consequences are identified, a plan is created to eliminate or reduce the risk and then the risk is prioritized.

What Does Data Have to Do with It?

In today's environment, risk management has become more important than ever, and by using analytics, you can identify the risks, analyze them, and determine what needs to be done about the risks.

Let's look at McDonalds. We talked about how they used data science earlier in the book. Of course, this is just an example, a completely made up scenario, but it can help us understand how data helps companies mitigate risks.

When it comes to a company like McDonalds, customer satisfaction is the number one priority as is with most companies today. Let's imagine that during the data collection, McDonalds finds that the average wait time for a customer in their drive thru is 3 minutes.

If this were a sit-down restaurant, this time would be great and there would be no need for risk assessment. However, let's also say that McDonalds found that the average customer waiting on a cup of coffee in the morning time waited for 3 minutes. This is obviously not going to keep customers happy.

After this data has been collected, it is time to find out why the customer is waiting in line for that long. Now it is time to look at a different set of data. Through doing this, the company finds that the issue is that there are not enough hash browns being prepared at a time, therefore, customers are having to wait in the line longer for the hash browns to cook.

This data is what allows the risk assessment manager to look at the problem and determine the risk. What is the risk? The first risk that would be looked at is unsatisfied customers, then lost customers, and customers leaving the line and orders being confused, which would lead to longer wait times.

Of course, this is not an extremely high risk issue but still one that would need to be resolved. Simple changes in how the stores are run could easily reduce the amount of time customers were waiting in the drive thru line.

This problem, no matter how small, could not have been handled had it not been through data analytics.

Now let's think about CVS, the pharmacy we talked about earlier. Through data collection, the company was able to understand that 40% of the driver accidents were happening at one specific location. This is a huge risk, because these accidents were not only leading to late deliveries and damaged docks but lawsuits from injured drivers, wrecks were being caused because the loading dock was so difficult to access, therefore leading to even more lawsuits from customers who had been involved in the accident.

Before this data was collected, the company had no idea that so many of these accidents were taking place in one area nor did they understand why the accidents were happening.

After the data was collected, the company was able to make the changes that they needed to make to reduce the amount of accidents that their drivers were getting involved in by 40%, while reducing costs enormously because of completely eliminating the risk of being sued, by eliminating the chance of drivers causing an accident.

Credit card companies use the data that they collect to determine which potential customers would pose a risk to their company when it comes to losses. This is often determined by credit score. Those with a low credit score are not likely to pay their credit card bills, which means that while the company could charge them interest on the money, it is not likely that they would ever be paid, especially without paying a collection agency to collect the money for them.

Insurance companies use the data they collect to determine what type of risk they would be taking if they insured specific customers, banks used the data that they have collected about their customers to determine their risks when providing loans, and so on.

By using data analytics, companies are able to identify risks before they become an issue, and this allows them to analyze the risk, investigate how they can eliminate the risk, and eliminate the risk completely.

Let's talk about a real time risk, one that needs attention right away and one that happens all of the time. On a regular basis, online companies will put out what are called coupon codes. These codes are meant to be put in a specific field during check out to get a specific discount.

What also happens on a regular basis is that these coupon codes take off much more than they are supposed to, often giving products away completely. With the advancements in technology and social media, 'glitches' such as this are shared quickly with hundreds of thousands of people.

Now even though you may be sitting there thinking that the risk for losing a large amount of money is low, you would be wrong. Let's say, for example, a company puts out a coupon code that is supposed to take 10% off of an order of $100 or more. But as it turns out, the code is taking 100% off an order of $100 dollars (This is not as far-fetched as one would think).

One person finds this and shares it in a group of 30,000 people, who share it within the groups they are part of and so on. Now if only those first 30,000 people made one purchase, the company would lose around 3 million dollars but fraud goes much further than that and it moves very quickly.

A mistake like this could cost a company 100 million dollars in a matter of minutes! This is where real time data collection comes into play. If the program notices a huge jump in sales, it can begin predicting what the profits are going to be. When the data shows that there is no profit, or that money is actually being lost, the company is able to quickly pull the code off line, stopping it from being used.

This also allows the company to cancel all of the previous orders that would have been shipped out had the risk not been identified and managed quickly.

This is becoming more and more important every single day as companies are becoming more aware of the fact that there are actually people out there searching for these mistakes, looking to take advantage of them, not caring about the damage that can be done to a company in a matter of minutes.

Fraud is one of the biggest reasons that many businesses are using data to focus on mitigating risks. It is becoming easier for people to crack systems, to crack codes, and to take advantage companies all over the world.

Chapter 13 - How to Get Started

Data analytics is not simple; it is not something that the average person is able to do, those who practice data analytics must have a Bachelor of Science degree.

Other requirements involved taking calculus 1 and 2, and statistics 2450, economics, linguistics, and the list goes on and on.

Data analytics is not something that someone without the proper education should attempt. It can be confusing, and if you do not have the proper education, you are simply not going to be able to understand the trends that are shown in the data.

Once a company has decided that they are ready to take on big data, there are specific steps that can be taken to make the entire process easier. The first thing that a company needs to know is that they need to start slow, not jumping in with both feet or being too ambitious.

Obtaining a cloud service is a great first step as it is easier to manage large amounts of data if done through a cloud service. Companies that relied on more traditional means of storing their data have in the past may be reluctant to use a cloud data service for fear of not being able to protect the data but the days of having to worry about data being shared through the cloud are long behind us. These types of services are just like any other business and even though it was a bit iffy when the companies first started out, today, the services are much safer.

You also need to understand that change can be scary. It is something humans will fight against, even though they know it is in their best interests, simply because they are afraid of what is going to happen. Fear of the unknown is what makes people afraid of change.

It is also important to understand that big data can exist within a company without changing the company so to speak. Many small companies are afraid of taking part in big data because they are afraid that it will force them to make changes they do not want to make.

The opposite is true. Even when you collect the data, analyze it, and understand what it is saying, you do not have to make any changes if you do not want to or do not feel the need.

Big data is going to help you understand what your customers need and want while helping to ensure you are able to reduce the risks you are taking in every part of your business.

If you really want your business to be successful, big data is the way to go. It is also important to understand that almost 90% of the data out there has been created in the past couple of years, and even though big data was first introduced years ago, it is quickly becoming the norm for all companies.

The three steps that need to be taken to start using big data in your business are to first start collecting the data. After the data is collected, you will need to determine how you will analyze the data. Most companies start off with descriptive analytics, simply allowing themselves to look at the trends of the past, and understand what caused those trends. By understanding those trends, the company can then plan to reproduce those patterns in the future, which is where predictive analytics comes in.

After all of this has been mastered, and the business is running well, prescriptive analytics can begin to be used to mitigate risks, help make decisions, and determine what is best for the company.

Big data and data analytics are not something that should be taken lightly. Instead, they are what can determine if your business is successful or not. It can mean the difference between earning a profit and losing your entire business. It is something that every company should be taking advantage of today.

Thanks again for reading this book and I hope it was able to help further your knowledge on data analytics. There is one favor I'd like to ask however, if you enjoyed the book would you be kind enough to leave a review on Amazon? It would be greatly appreciated!

Go Here to Leave a Review:

https://www.amazon.com/dp/B01HQFEWKU/

Till next time,
James Smith

Made in the USA
Middletown, DE
15 July 2016